Steadwell Books World Tour

BRAZIL

ADRIANA DOMINGUEZ

Steadwell Books

Raintree Steck-Vaughn Publishers
A Harcourt Company

Austin · New York
www.raintreesteckvaughn.com

Published by Raintree Steck-Vaughn Publishers, an imprint of Steck-Vaughn Company.

Editor: Simone T. Ribke
Designer: Maria E. Torres

Library of Congress Cataloging-in-Publication Data
Dominguez, Adriana.
  Brazil / by Adriana Dominguez.
    p. cm. -- (Steadwell books world tour)
  Summary: Describes the history, geography, economy, government, religious and social life, languages and cultures, various famous people, and outstanding tourist sites of Brazil. Includes a recipe for pudim de leite, a flan.
  ISBN 0-7398-4709-0
    1. Brazil--Juvenile literature. [1. Brazil.] I. Title. II. Series.

  F2508.5 .D66 2002
  918.1--dc21   2002017863

Printed in the United States of America
1 2 3 4 5 6 7 8 9 10 WZ 07 06 05 04 03 02

Photo acknowledgments
Cover (a) ©Haroldo de Faria Castro/Getty Images; cover (b) ©Reuters NewMedia Inc/ CORBIS; cover (c) © Dave G. Houser/Houserstock; p.1a © Jacues Jangoux; p.1b © Stephanie Maze/CORBIS; p.1c © Staffan Widstrand/CORBIS; p.3a © Reuters NewMedia Inc/CORBIS; p.3b ©Jacues Jangoux; p.5 ©Karl Kummels/SuperStock; p.6 ©Nik Wheeler/CORBIS; p.7 ©Jonathan Blair/CORBIS; p.8 ©Karl Kummels/SuperStock; p.13 ©Jacues Jangoux; p.14 ©Jeremy Horner/ CORBIS; p.16 ©Haroldo de Faria Castro/Getty Images; p.19 ©Dave G. Houser/Houserstock; p.21a ©Owen Franken/CORBIS; p.21b ©Tom Brakefield/CORBIS; p.23 ©Rogerio Reis/Latin Focus; p.25a ©John Langford; p.25b ©Joe McDonald/CORBIS; p.27,28 ©Stephanie Maze/CORBIS; p.29 ©J.R. Couto/Latin Focus; p.31a ©Julian Calder/CORBIS; p.31b © Marcelo Soubhia/Latin Focus; p.34,35 ©Steven Mark Needham/FoodPix/Getty Images; p.37a ©Staffan Widstrand/CORBIS; p.37b ©Victor Englebert/Photo Researchers, Inc.; p.38a ©Jacues Jangoux/Getty Images; p.40 ©Stephanie Maze/CORBIS; p.43b ©Jacues Jangoux; p.44a, 44b ©TimePix; p.44c ©Moshe Shai/CORBIS.

Additional Photography by Comstock Royalty Free, PhotoDisc, and the Steck-Vaughn Collection.

CONTENTS

Welcome to Brazil

Are you planning a trip to Brazil? Maybe you just like to learn about different countries. Brazil is a great place to visit. It has world-famous celebrations. It is home to one of the most mysterious and beautiful rain forests. There are tall mountains, sandy beaches, and exciting cities. Want to know more about this fascinating country? Read on!

Reader's Tips

- *Use the Table of Contents*

Do you already know what you are looking for? Maybe you just want to know what topics this book will cover. The Contents page tells you what topics you will read about. It tells you where to find them in the book.

- *Look at the Pictures*

This book has lots of great photos. Flip through and check out those pictures you like the best. This is a great way to get a quick idea of what this book is all about. Read the captions to learn even more about the photos.

- *Use the Index*

If you are looking for a certain fact, then you might want to turn to the Index at the back of the book. The Index lists the subjects covered in the book. It will tell you what pages to find them on.

▲ BRASILIA
Brasilia isn't the biggest city in Brazil, but it is the capital. This modern city is home to Brazil's government.

BRAZIL'S PAST

Do you know where Brazilians come from? Why do they speak Portuguese? Reading about the country's history will give you answers to these and other questions.

Early History

Not much is known about the **Native** Americans who lived in Brazil before the Europeans discovered it. We do know that most of them were Tupí-Guaraní. The Tupí-Guaraní lived off their small crops. There were between two and five million Native Americans when European first came to Brazil.

Discovery by the Portuguese

In A.D. 1500, an explorer named Pedro Alvares Cabral sailed from Lisbon, Portugal, to look for a **trade route** to India. Instead, he found Brazil. King João III of Portugal sent the first settlers there in 1531.

The first settlers were Portuguese criminals. They lived with the native Tupís and learned to speak their language. The natives taught them how to farm and hunt. Settlers and natives also married each other.

◀ **KNIGHTS IN SHINING ARMOR**
Native Tupí Indians were no match for Portuguese soldiers wearing armor and riding horses.

The settlers noticed that Brazil was a perfect place for growing sugar cane. Sugar is made from sugar cane. For most of the 1500s, the native Tupís worked as slaves on the sugar **plantations**. Many slaves died from hard labor and European diseases. In the 1600s, the Portuguese brought African slaves to Brazil to replace the Native Americans. Marriages among Europeans, Tupís, and Africans are one reason modern Brazil is made up of so many different cultures.

In 1807, the French emperor Napoleon conquered Portugal. The Portuguese royal family escaped to Brazil. King João VI went back to Portugal after Napoleon left in 1821. His son Pedro stayed in Brazil. In 1822, Pedro was crowned Constitutional Emperor of Brazil.

▲ BRASILIA'S TOWERS
The Brazilian congress meets in these tall buildings.

The "Old Republic"

In the 1800s, coffee became more important than sugar cane. The owners of coffee plantation became very rich. They wanted slavery to continue. They did not want the emperor to control their country after he **abolished** slavery in 1888.

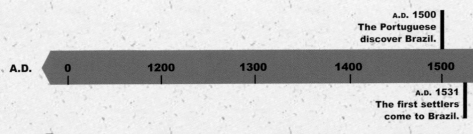

A.D. 1500
The Portuguese
discover Brazil.

A.D.   0   1200   1300   1400   1500

A.D. 1531
The first settlers
come to Brazil.

In 1889, General Manuel Deodoro da Fonseca led a revolt that overthrew the Brazilian emperor. He declared Brazil a **republic**. Manuel Deodoro da Fonseca was elected its first president.

Brazil Today

The 20th century was very hard for Brazil. The government was not always **democratic**. The "Second Republic" was created in 1945. The Military took control of Brazil in 1964. Brazil became a democracy again in 1984. Brazil's first capital was Salvador, on the eastern coast. Today, the capital is Brasilia.

Many of Brazil's problems continue. Brazil owes money to other countries. Many people in Brazil are very poor while others are very rich. Some people worry about how the government plans to help the country. But now that Brazilians can vote for their leaders, many think that Brazil has a bright future.

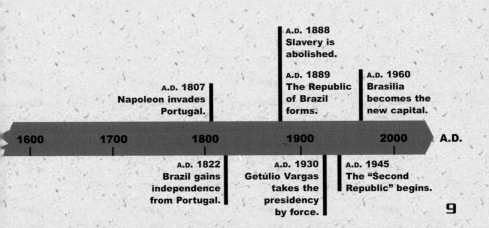

A.D. 1888
Slavery is abolished.

A.D. 1889
The Republic of Brazil forms.

A.D. 1960
Brasilia becomes the new capital.

A.D. 1807
Napoleon invades Portugal.

1600   1700   1800   1900   2000   A.D.

A.D. 1822
Brazil gains independence from Portugal.

A.D. 1930
Getúlio Vargas takes the presidency by force.

A.D. 1945
The "Second Republic" begins.

9

A LOOK AT BRAZIL'S GEOGRAPHY

Brazil is so famous for its forests that its name even came from its trees. The Portuguese named the land for its beautiful brasilwood trees, which are still found in the Amazon rain forests. The Amazon rain forest makes up 30% of all the rain forests in the entire world! Many people visit Brazil to take ecological tours of the rain forest. Ecological tours show people the different animals and plants that live in a place.

Land

Most of Brazil's land is low and flat. It is almost impossible to think of Brazil without thinking of the Amazon rain forest—it's huge! A rain forest is a place where trees and plants grow tall and close together—and of course, it rains a lot. Rain forest covers almost half of Brazil. It stretches 2,300,000 square miles (6,000,000 sq km), from the north to western and central Brazil.

There are several mountain ranges along the Atlantic coast. The tallest mountain, called Pico de Bandeira, is 9,495 feet (2,894 m) tall. The mountains in Brazil are not the tallest in the world. However, the Brazilian mountains that rise next to the ocean are awesome in their beauty.

BRAZIL'S SIZE ▶

Brazil is the fifth-largest country in the world and the largest country in South America. It covers 3,286,474 square miles (8,511,965 sq km). Brazil is so large that it borders every country in South America except Chile and Ecuador!

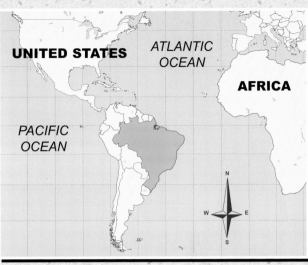

BRAZIL

★ National Capital
● Major Cities
— Rivers

0 200 400 Kilometers
0   200   400 Miles

Water

Brazil has the largest river in the world, the Amazon River. It is not as long as the Nile River in Africa, but it holds much more water. The Amazon River is in the northern part of the country. It flows east to the Alantic Ocean. It travels right through the Amazon rain forest. The Amazon and the rivers that connect to it provide water for most of the plants and animals that live in the rain forest.

Another amazing site in Brazil is the Iguaçu Falls. The falls lie along the Argentina-Paraguay border in the south. They are over 2 miles (3.2 km) wide, and average 200 feet (61 m) high!

Brazil is also known for its beautiful beaches, and there are plenty of them—the country's coastline is 4,600 miles (7,400 km) long. And since much of Brazil lies along the **equator**, the sun is very strong. So bring plenty of sunblock!

BRAZIL

★ National Capital
• Major City
— Rivers

ATLANTIC OCEAN

Rio Negro
Amazon R.
Amazon R.
Rio Madeira

Brasília ★

Iguaçu Falls

▲ **THE MIGHTY AMAZON**
The great Amazon River winds through Brazil. It is surrounded by lush, green rain forest.

◀ IT'S RAINING...
Pack an umbrella
when going to
Brazil. It may be
hot, but it rains
often.

Weather

If you like warm weather, then Brazil's climate is as close to perfect as you can get. Most of the country does not get cold. The region around the Amazon rain forest is close to the equator. The average temperature there stays around 80 degrees Fahrenheit (27° C). Rain forests are also very **humid** and get far more rain than anywhere else. That's why they are called rain forests.

Brazil is on the opposite side of the equator from the United States or Europe. The U.S. and Europe are located at the top half of the globe, above the equator. Brazil is below the equator, in the southern half of the globe. So when it is winter in New York or England, it is summer in Brazil.

RIO DE JANEIRO TOP-10 CHECKLIST

Here is a list of the top 10 things you should do if you go to Rio.

☐ Walk the busy area around Copacabana Beach.

☐ Take a cable car to the top of Sugar Loaf Mountain.

☐ Check out the 5-ton (4,536-kg) meteorite at the National Museum.

☐ Visit the zoo in Quinta Da Boã Vista.

☐ Look at the Brazilian landmarks around Praça Quinze.

☐ Listen to street musicians and have a picnic in Largo do Boticário.

☐ See the ruins of old mansions in Parque das Ruinas in Santa Teresa.

☐ Spend some time at Nossa Senhora da Glória do Outeiro church.

☐ See a play or have dinner at the Teatro Paço Imperial.

☐ Go to Maracaná Stadium and watch a soccer game.

4 TOP SIGHTS

Brazil is a very large country. Even people who live there have not seen it all. Here are some suggestions to help you experience the best of what Brazil has to offer.

The Amazon River

People called caboclos live in the towns along the banks of the Amazon River. The caboclos live off the **natural resources** of the rain forest.

Lots and lots of animals live in the rain forest. Many of them go to the Amazon River to drink its water or to catch prey. Did you know that you could see a dolphin in a river? Well, in the Amazon River you can! The tucuxi dolphin lives there. It is the smallest dolphin in the world. Fish like piranhas and electric eels also live in the river. Beware of the piranhas—these fish like to eat fresh meat. And electric eels can really give you a shock.

Many different **species** of colorful bird live in the trees. These include toucans, parrots, and hummingbirds. Do you like bugs? Great! Because there are over 1,800 species of butterfly and more than 200 species of mosquito in the rain forest. (You might want to bring some bug repellent so those mosquitoes will leave you alone.)

All of these animals depend on the Amazon River for their survival. The Amazon River is not just a river—it is a source of life.

▼ LIFE ON THE AMAZON

Below, a young boy rows a dugout canoe through thick jungle. Many Native Americans still live along the Amazon River.

TAPIR CALF ▶

A baby tapir is born with stripes and dots. This pattern helps to hide it from danger. The patterns will disappear as the calf gets older.

Salvador da Bahia

Salvador da Bahia is a city loaded with historic buildings and amazing beaches. It was Brazil's capital until the 1960s. It sits between green tropical hills and the bay of Todos los Santos. The city was built on two levels. Buildings and houses were built on the hills. The forts, docks, and warehouses were built on the beaches. Electric elevators, called Elevador Lacerda, carry more than 50,000 passengers from one level of the city to the other every day. They go up and down 279 feet (85 m) in less than 15 seconds!

Salvador was founded in 1549 and remained Brazil's most important city for 300 years. It was famous for its beautiful mansions and churches trimmed with gold. The city has 34 colonial churches. Visit some and you can almost feel Brazilian history.

African culture can be tasted, seen, and enjoyed throughout this city and all of Brazil during the Carnival festival each year. Tourists from all over the world travel to see the Carnival festivals. There are parades, music, food, and more—each shares a mix of African and Brazilian culture. If you can't make it to Carnival, you can still learn about Brazilian African culture. Salvador's Museu Afro-Brasileira a museum that you can learn from at any time of year.

▲ A PARTY TO REMEMBER

Carnival is one of the greatest parties in the world! This amazing five-day festival will dazzle you with floats, samba dancers, Afro-Brazilian music, and much, much more.

GOING TO SCHOOL IN BRAZIL

Kids in Brazil go to school between the ages of 7 and 14. After they turn 14, many children leave school to help at home. Others stay in high school and may go on to college.

Brazilian schools are very similar to schools in the United States. Students study math, science, and history—all the basics—at public or private schools. Classes in Brazil are taught in Portuguese, the national language. There are many private international schools in Brazil. International schools often teach classes in a language other than Portuguese, such as English or German. There are also religious private schools. Most religious schools are Catholic.

▲ AT SCHOOL IN BRAZIL...
These kids are learning many of the same subjects as you do. Classes are taught in Portuguese, the national language.

If you like soccer, you probably know about Brazil's national soccer team. In Brazil, soccer is called futebol (which sounds just like football). The national team has won the highest soccer prize, the World Cup, four times. Brazilians are very proud of their team. They like to play soccer almost as much as they like to talk about it!

Brazilians play many other sports, too. Car racing, horse racing, tennis, volleyball, and water polo are all very popular there. Brazilians also like to play a game called boliche, which is lawn bowling. In lawn bowling, players use several heavy black or brown balls.

▲ SOCCER STADIUM
Soccer, called futebol, is one of the country's favorite sports. If you can play it, or even talk about it, you will make friends right away.

FROM FARMING TO FACTORIES

When the Portuguese first came to Brazil, they noticed that the land and climate were perfect for growing sugar cane. Later, they grew coffee. Many discovered that they could make more money from it than from sugar. Brazil's land is still very rich today, and farming is still important. Farmed products, including coffee, bring in a lot of money to Brazil's **economy**. The kind of money people use in Brazil is called the real.

The Amazon rain forest is very important to the country's economy. Trees are used for **timber**. The land is used to raise cattle, among other things. Many people in Brazil and all over the world are trying to stop the destruction of the rain forest. Yet beef and timber are very important to Brazil's economy, so this is not easy to do.

Like the rest of the world, Brazil is becoming more modern. Today, fewer Brazilians are farmers. More people work in factories. Brazilian factories make **textiles**, shoes, chemicals, planes, cars, and car parts. These export products are sold to other countries.

There are many poor people in Brazil—in fact, almost 50% of all Brazilians live in **poverty**. In Brazil, the poor people are very poor. The rich are very rich. The government is working to help its poor people live better lives.

COFFEE BEANS ▶
The beans are
dried and specially
prepared. They are
then ground and
brewed into coffee.

▼ **A CAR FACTORY**
Brazilian workers on an assembly line put the finishing touches
on new automobiles. Many will be exported—sent to other
countries for sale.

THE BRAZILIAN GOVERNMENT

Brazil's government is a republic. In a republic, you vote for members of the government. Brazil's government is made up of three different parts, or branches. These three parts are called the executive, legislative, and judicial branches.

The executive branch is made up of the president, vice president, and the cabinet. The president and vice president are elected by the people and serve for four years. The cabinet is a group of people the president chooses to help him or her. The executive branch makes sure that laws are obeyed.

The legislative branch is the National Congress, which makes, the laws. It is made up of the Federal Senate and the Chamber of Deputies. The judicial branch is made up of judges. They make sure that the laws are fair.

BRAZIL'S NATIONAL FLAG

The flag of Brazil has a green background with a large yellow diamond in the center. In the middle of the diamond is a blue circle. It has 27 stars and a banner. On the banner is written "Ordem e Progresso," which means "Order and Progress." The green color stands for the lush fields and forests of Brazil. The yellow diamond represents the country's gold supply. The blue circle with the 27 stars stands for the night sky over Brazil's capital and its 26 states.

RELIGIONS OF BRAZIL

About 80% of Brazilians are Catholic. Catholics practice a form of the Christian religion. Christians follow the teachings of Jesus as written in the New Testament of the Bible. Today, nearly every town in Brazil has a church. Catholics follow a religious leader called the Pope.

The number of Protestants in Brazil has also grown. Protestantism is now the second most important religion in the country. Protestantism is another form of Christianity. They do not follow the Pope.

Other religious groups, such as Jews and Buddhists, make up about 3% to 5% of Brazil's population. Candomblé is a religion that was created by African slaves. It mixes African and Christian beliefs. In recent years, it has become more popular.

BRAZIL'S CHURCHES ▶
European colonists founded many of Brazil's oldest Catholic churches. These historic churches are still in use today.

BRAZILIAN FOOD

Are you used to fast food? Then you will have to slow down a little in Brazil. Brazilians like to take the time to sit back and enjoy their meals. Breakfast is the only small and quick meal they eat. A typical Brazilian breakfast is coffee or milk, bread and jam, fresh fruit, and sometimes cheese and ham.

Papayas and mangoes are grown in Brazil. They are extra sweet and juicy, so make sure you have some while you're there!

Lunch or dinner is the time to sit down, relax, and talk with family and friends. Dinner is usually eaten well into the night. The meals are large and there is often a lot to choose from.

If you like beef, you will love Brazilian barbecues! Although barbecues are very popular, the national dish of Brazil is feijoada. It is Brazilian black beans in a stew, with lots of beef and sausage in it, too. Even if you are very full, don't skip dessert! You'll regret not having the Brazilian-style flan that is a delicious custard.

◀ FEIJOADA
Brazilian-style black beans are a favorite choice in homes and restaurants.

BRAZILIAN-STYLE FLAN

Ingredients:
1 cup sugar (for the caramel)
1 can sweetened condensed milk
Equal amount of regular milk
(use the can from the condensed
    milk to measure)
3 eggs
8-inch ring mold
Roasting pan

WARNING:
**Never cook or bake by yourself.
Always have an adult assist you
in the kitchen.**

Directions:
Place 1 to 2 inches (2.5 to 5 cm) of water in a roasting pan.
Have an adult help you place the pan in the oven and preheat to
325° F. Put the sugar in the ring mold. Have an adult help you
place the mold on the stove, over medium heat. Have an adult
help you to keep turning the mold until the sugar melts into a
golden brown caramel. Be careful not to burn the sugar or
yourself (use oven mitts to hold the mold). Take the caramel out
of the mold. Let the mold cool. Combine the condensed milk,
regular milk, and eggs in a blender, and whip until smooth. Pour
this mixture into the mold and place it in the center of the roasting
pan holding the water. Bake for about 1 hour. Let it cool to room
temperature and place in refrigerator, preferably overnight (at least
6 hours). Place a deep platter over the mold and turn it over: the
flan should slide out easily. If it doesn't, give the mold a firm,
careful shake. Spoon the caramel sauce on top and serve.

UP CLOSE: SAVING THE RAIN FOREST

Why Is the Amazon Rain Forest in Danger?

Even though they are so important to all life on Earth, tropical rain forests are being destroyed at an alarming rate.

Logging is a big problem in the Amazon rain forest. Scientists think that about 10% of the trees in the Amazon rain forest have already been cut down by logging companies. These companies look for valuable types of wood found only in the rain forest. If left alone, the trees in these areas may grow again on their own.

After the logging companies cut down all the trees in one area, poor farmers take over. They burn the remaining plants and shrubs to clear the land for planting. This is called "slash and burn" agriculture. With none of its natural trees, plants, and animals, the soil loses its **nutrients**. After only a couple of years, the farmers can no longer use the soil to grow crops. They sell the land to ranchers or large plantation owners.

Ranchers use the land to grow cattle. Plantation owners use it to grow large-scale crops. When nothing more can be done with it, the land is abandoned. Without help from humans, the rain forest land becomes useless.

The worst part of this whole cycle is that it is not happening in just one part of the rain forest. More and more of the rain forest is being destroyed forever, every day.

LEARNING THE LANGUAGE

English	Portuguese	How to say it
Hello	Olá	OH-lah
Good day	Bon dia	bohn DEE-ah
Goodbye	Tchau	CHOW
My name is ___	Meu nome___	MEH-oo NOH-meh
What's your name?	Como é seu nome	KO-mo EH SHE-oo NOH-meh
See you later	Até logo	AH-tay LOW-go
Do you speak English?	Fala inglês	FAH-la in-GLAYSH

QUICK FACTS

BRAZIL

Capital ▶
Brasilia

Borders
Argentina, Bolivia,
Colombia, French Guiana,
Guyana, Paraguay,
Peru, Suriname, Uruguay,
and Venezuela

Area
8,511,965 square miles
(3,286,474 sq km)

Population
172,860,370

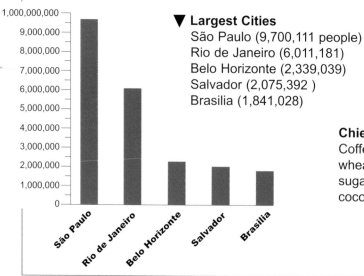

▼ Largest Cities
São Paulo (9,700,111 people)
Rio de Janeiro (6,011,181)
Belo Horizonte (2,339,039)
Salvador (2,075,392)
Brasilia (1,841,028)

Chief Crops
Coffee, soybeans,
wheat, rice, corn,
sugar cane,
cocoa, citrus, beef

▲ Flag of Brazil

Coastline
7,491 miles (4,654 km)

Longest River ▶
Amazon River
3,900 miles (6,276 km)

Literacy Rate
83% of all Brazilians
can read

Major Industries
Textiles, shoes, chemicals,
cement, lumber, iron ore,
tin, steel, aircraft,
motor vehicles and parts,
other machinery
and equipment

Natural Resources
Bauxite, gold, iron ore,
manganese, nickel,
phosphates, platinum, tin,
uranium, petroleum,
hydropower, timber

◀ **Monetary Unit**
Real

PEOPLE TO KNOW

Many people have made Brazil the fascinating place that it is. Here are a few to find out more about.

◀ PÉLÉ

Pélé's name is Edson Arantes do Nascimento. You might have heard of him if you like soccer. At the height of his career, he was the most famous athlete in the world! He led the Brazilian national team to three World Cup victories.

SONIA BRAGA ▶

Sonia Braga started her acting career at the young age of 14. She is one of Brazil's top actresses. One of her most famous roles was the 1985 American film *Kiss of the Spider Woman*. Sonia Braga has performed in films and television programs both in Brazil and the U.S.

◀ ANTONIO JOBIM

Antonio Carlos Jobim was one of the founders of the famous bossa nova movement in music. He was born in Rio de Janeiro in 1927 and died in New York in 1994. Jobim composed many famous songs, including "The Girl from Ipanema."

MORE TO READ

Want to know more about Brazil? Check out the books below.

Ancona, George. *Carnival*. New York: Harcourt Inc,. 1999. This book shows you how the small town of Olinda in Brazil celebrates Carnival. It has great pictures that will make you feel like you're in the middle of it all!

Haverstock, Nathan A. *Brazil—in Pictures*. Minneapolis, MN: Lerner Publishing Group, 1997. This books tells about the land, history, government, people, and economy of the country—in pictures.

Lippert, Margaret H. *The Sea Serpent's Daughter: A Brazilian Legend*. Mahwah, NJ: Troll Communications, 1993. This book retells the Brazilian legend of how the Sea Serpent's gift of darkness to his daughter brings night to the people of the rain forest.

Lourie, Peter and Marcos Santilli. *Amazon: A Young Reader's Look at the Last Frontier*. Honesdale, PA: Boyds Mills Press, 1988. A writer and a photographer travel through the Amazon to show you its secrets and tell you why we need to save this important part of the world.

GLOSSARY

Abolished (uh-BOL-isht)—put an official end to something

Bay (BAY)—a wide opening in the shoreline, where the sea is fairly quiet

Conservation (kon-sur-VAY-shun)—protection of nature such as wildlife and rain forests

Democratic (dem-oh-CRAT-ic)—responsible to all the people, not just a small group

Economy (i-KON-uh-mee)—a country's way of running its industry, trade, and money

Equator (i-KWAY-tur)—an imaginary line along the middle of Earth, halfway between the North and South poles

Extinct (ek-STINGKT)—no longer in existence; all members of a group have died out

Humid (HYOO-mid)—damp and moist

Jury (JUR-ee)—a group of people who judge an event

Logging (LOGG-ing)—cutting down many trees at a time

Native (NAY-tiv)—born in a certain place or country

Natural resources (NACH-ur-uhl REE-sor-sez)— water, plants, wildlife, minerals, and other things found in nature that are of use to people

Nutrients (NOO-tree-uhnts)—parts of the soil that cause things to grow

Plantations (plan-TAY-shuhnz)—large farms that grow crops, where the workers live on the land

Port (PORT)—a place where boats can safely dock to load and unload cargo

Poverty (POV-ur-tee)—not having enough money for decent food, clothing, and shelter

Preserves (pri-ZURVZ)—places such as parklands that are kept in their original state

Republic (ri-PUB-lik)—a country with a form of government in which people vote for their leaders

Sea level (SEE LEV-uhl)—the average level of the ocean's surface, used for measuring the height or depth of another place

Species (SPEE-sheez)—groups of animals or plants that have similar traits and can produce fertile offspring

Textiles (TEK-stilez)—cloth or fabric that has been woven or knitted

Timber (TIM-bur)—wood that has been cut for people's use

Trade Route (TRADE ROOT)—the path traders took to travel to and from Asia to buy goods and sell them in Europe; the trade route covered land, sea, and the important cities traders rested in along the way.

INDEX